SHAPES
AROUND ME

Illustrator: Sue Hendra
Editor: Amanda Askew
Designer: Susi Martin

Educational consultant:
Jillian Harker

Published in the United States by
QEB Publishing, Inc.
3 Wrigley, Suite A
Irvine, CA 92628

www.qed-publishing.co.uk

A CIP record for this book is available from the Library of Congress.

ISBN 978 1 59566 861 5 (paperback)

Printed in China

SHAPES
AROUND ME

Anita Loughrey

QEB Publishing

What is a circle?

This is a circle. A circle is a round shape with no corners.

Follow your finger around...

the edge of the circle.

Who is holding the circle kite?

Sam

John

Jenny

Counting circles

Point to the circles in the pictures.

How many circles does the caterpillar's body have?

Look out of the window. Can you see any circle shapes?

How many yellow circles does the flower have?

Answer: 6 circles

Colored circles

Circles can be different colors.

blue
green
yellow
red

How many blue circles can you see?

How many red circles can you see?

How many green circles can you see?

How many yellow circles can you see?

Drawing circles

Find a clean sheet of paper. Ask a grown-up to help you draw this plate of cupcakes.

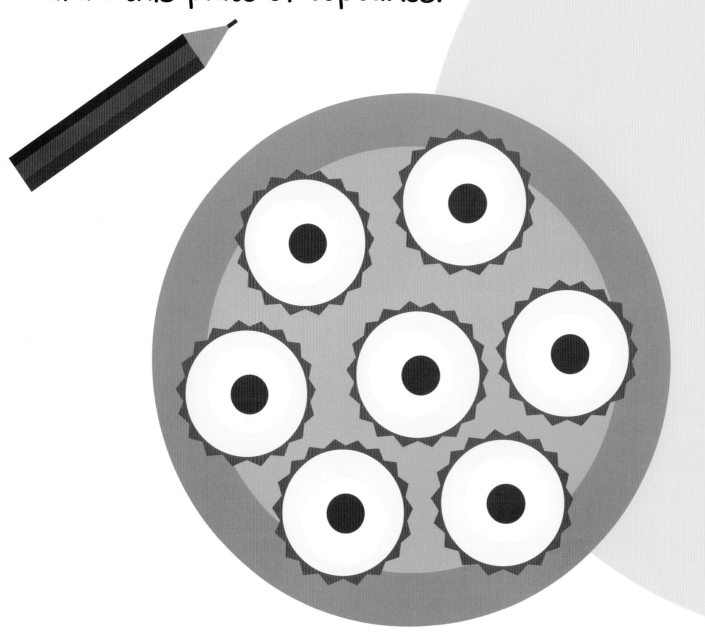

Next, see if you can draw a tree with red apples like this one.

Circles in the sandbox

Point to the circles in the picture.
Can you spot them all?

pail

sun

sunhat

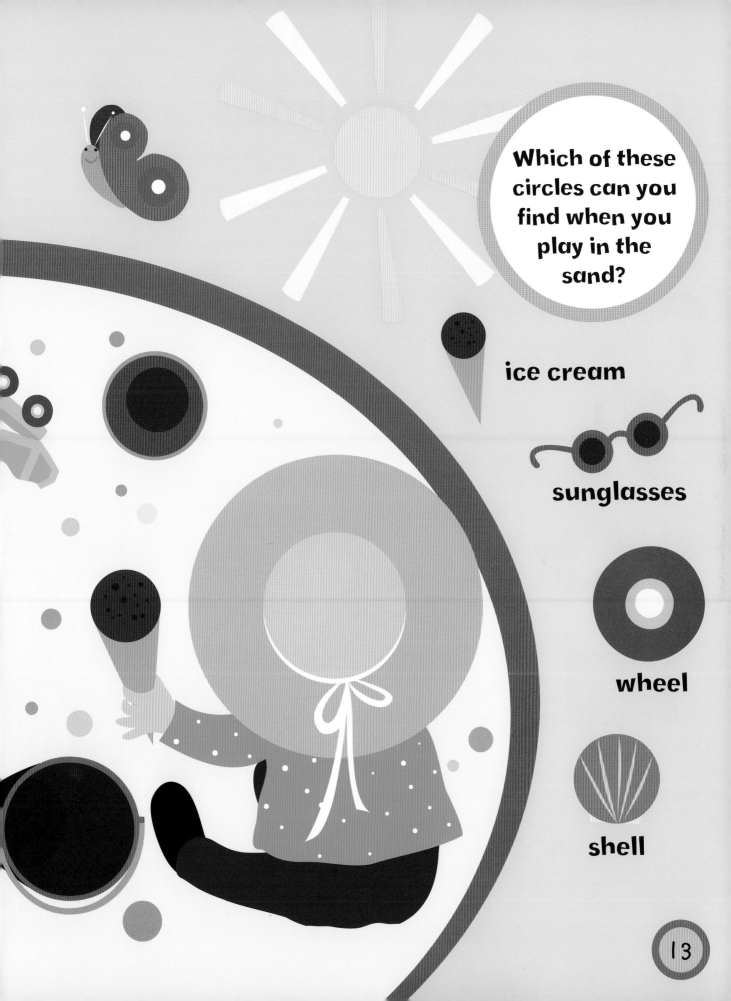

Which of these circles can you find when you play in the sand?

ice cream

sunglasses

wheel

shell

13

Circles at playtime

Point to the circles
in the picture.
Which ones have
you played with?

soccer ball

tire

basketball

Which of these circles can you find in your playground?

merry-go-round

tennis racket

hoop

15

Circles in the yard

Point to the circles.
Which circle is the
biggest?

parasol

apple

hose

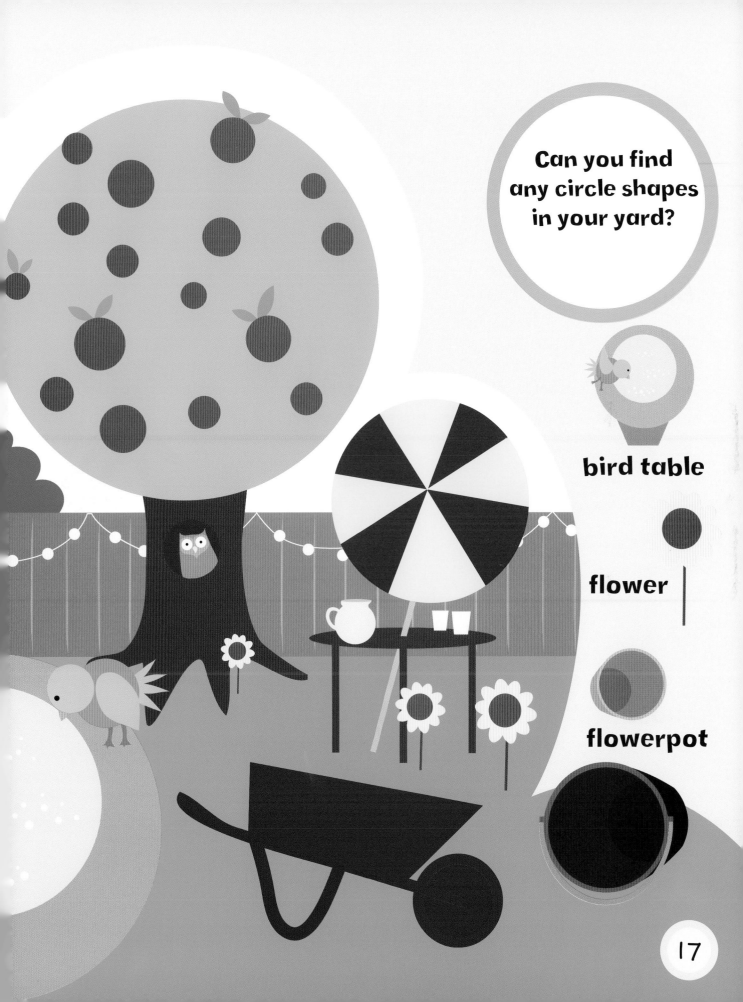

Can you find any circle shapes in your yard?

bird table

flower

flowerpot

17

What is a square?

This is a square. A square has four sides that are the same, and four corners.

Follow your finger around...

the edge of the square.

Who lives in the house with **square** windows?

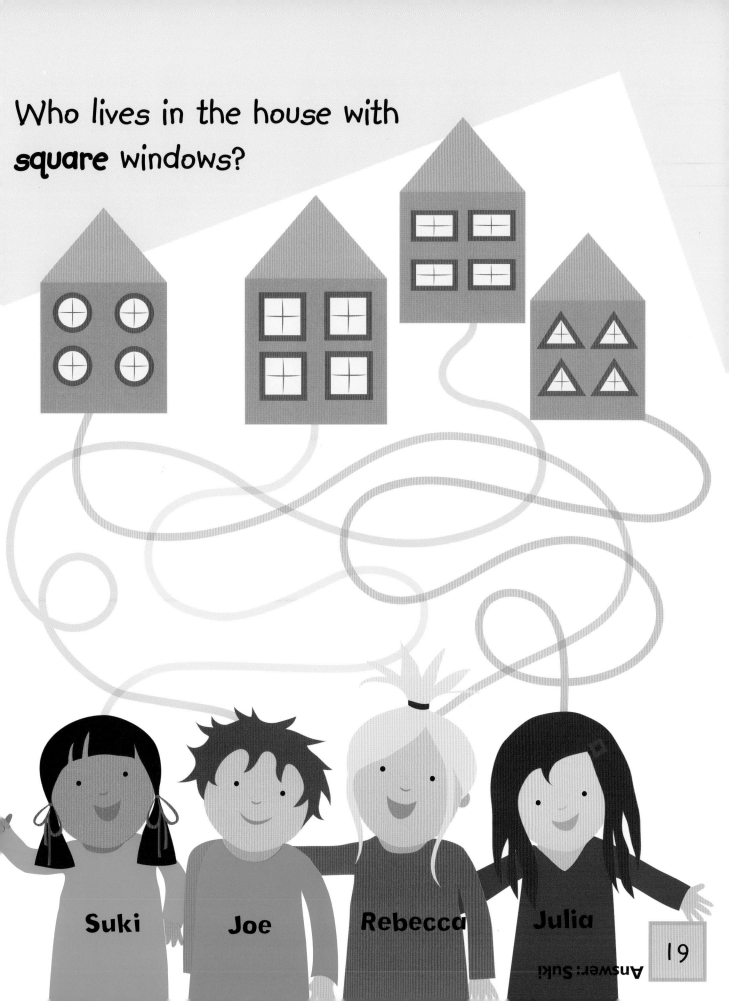

Suki

Joe

Rebecca

Julia

Colored squares

Squares can be different colors.

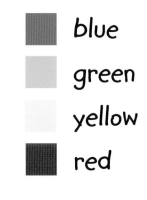

- blue
- green
- yellow
- red

How many blue squares can you see?

How many green squares can you see?

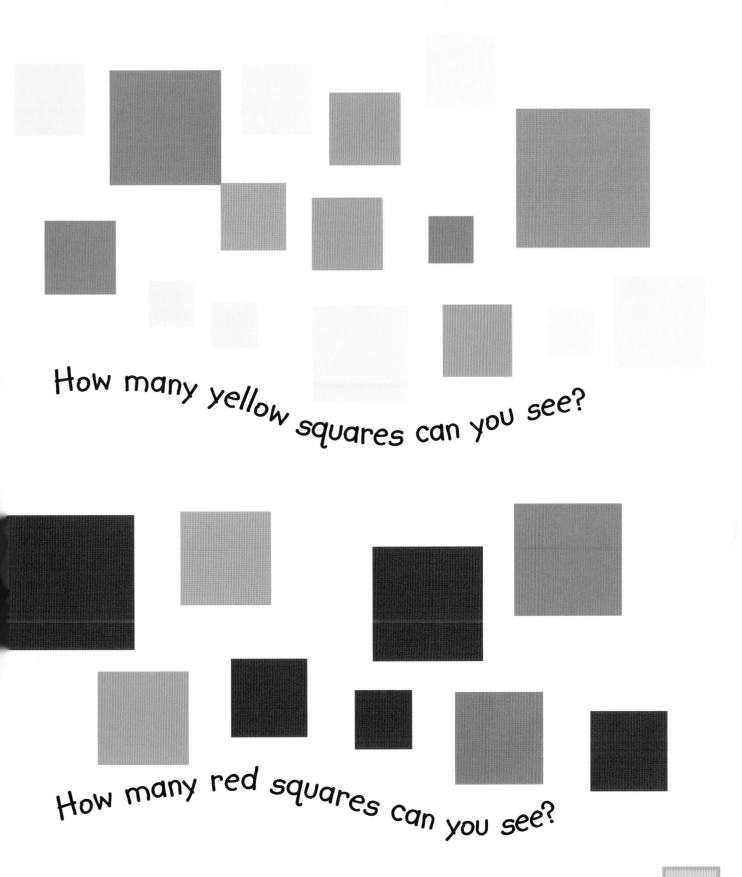

How many yellow squares can you see?

How many red squares can you see?

Counting squares

How many squares does the car pass by to get to the farm stall?

① ② ③ ④ ⑤ ⑥ ⑦ ⑧ ⑨ 10

Look out of your window. Point to any square shapes you can see.

Answer: 8 squares

Drawing squares

Find a clean sheet of paper. Ask a grown-up to help you draw a house with square windows.

Next, see if you can draw a square gift like this one.

Happy Birthday

Squares in the city

Point to the squares in the picture. Can you spot them all?

window

shopping bag

sign

planter

Gorgeous Gifts

Can you see any of these square shapes when you go out?

garbage

camera

drain

27

Squares at school

Point to the squares in the picture. Are there more than eight squares?

jigsaw puzzle

paintbox

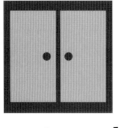

cupboard

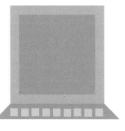

computer

What squares can you see in your class?

bulletin board

painting

toybox

29

Squares in the living room

Point to the squares in the picture. Which squares are small?

television

light switch

fireplace

picture

What square shapes can you see in your living room?

lamp

cushion

vase

31

What is a triangle?

A triangle has three straight edges and three corners.

Follow your finger around...

the edge of the triangle.

Who is going to the **triangle** tent?

Susi Jane Peter

Answer: Peter

Counting triangles

Point to the triangles in the picture.

How many triangles are there
on each of the lion's feet?

Answer: 6 triangles

How many triangle leaves does the tree have?

Answer: 10 triangles

Colored triangles

blue

green

yellow

red

Triangles can be different colors.

How many blue triangles can you see?

How many green triangles can you see?

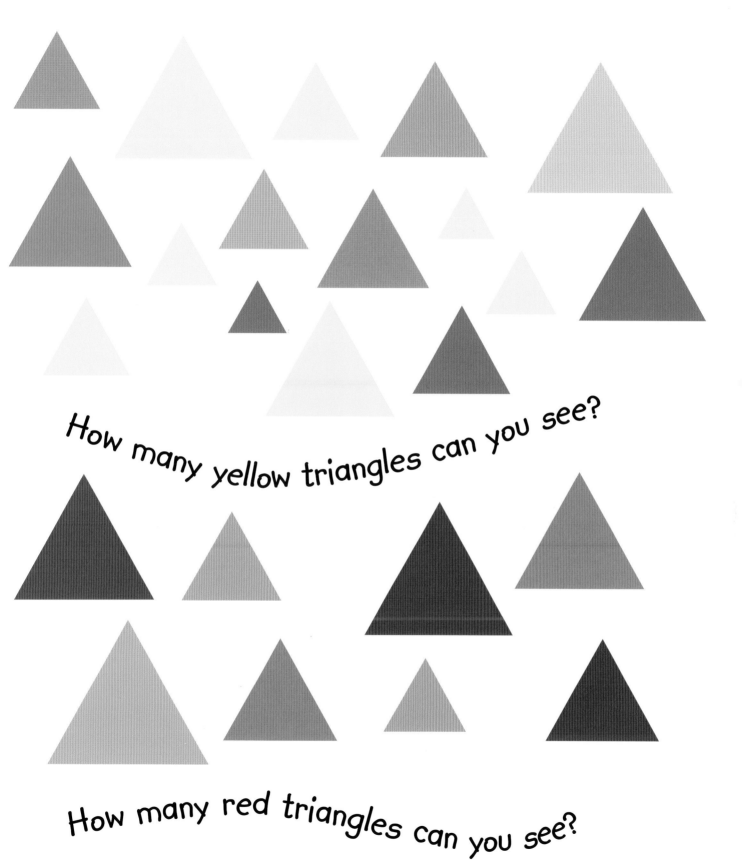

How many yellow triangles can you see?

How many red triangles can you see?

Drawing triangles

Find a clean sheet of paper.
Ask a grown-up
to help you
to draw this
sailboat.

Next, see if you can draw a kite like this one.

Triangles at the lake

Point to all the triangles in the picture. Can you spot them all?

kite

ice-cream cone

oar

Which of these triangle shapes have you seen?

wing

hat

sail

Triangles at the zoo

Point to all the triangles in the picture.

wing

horn

tooth

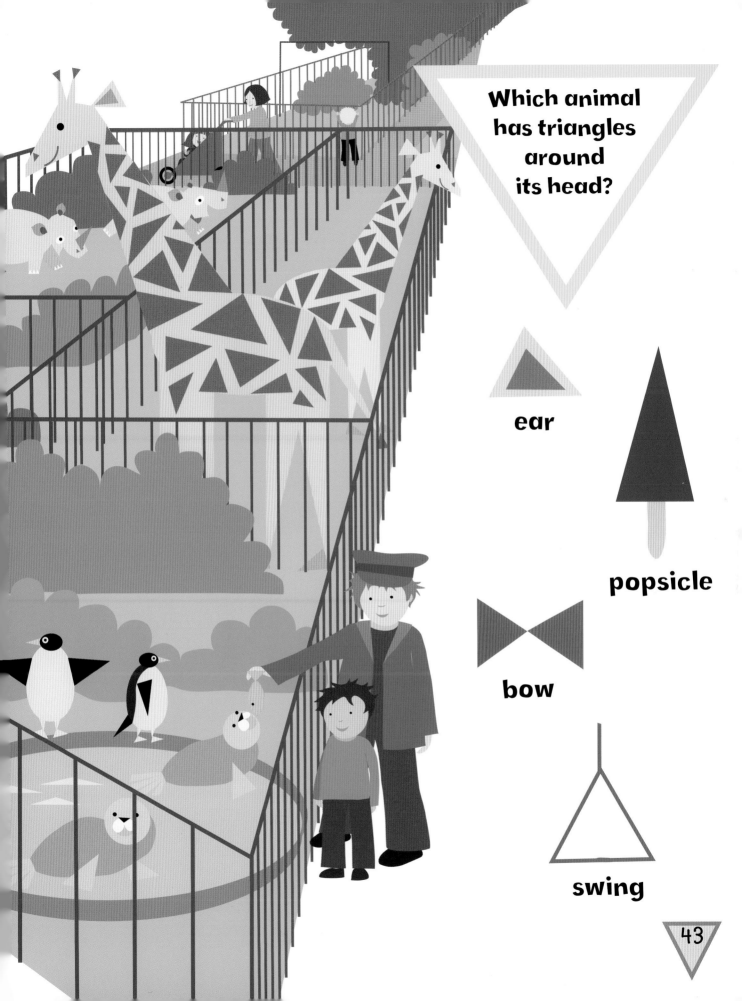

Which animal has triangles around its head?

ear

popsicle

bow

swing

43

Party triangles

Point to all the triangles in the picture. Which ones have you seen at a party?

present

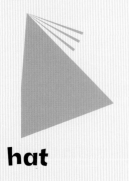

hat

cake

Which of these triangle foods have you eaten?

button

paper napkin

sandwich

pizza

Know your shapes

Look back through the
pages of your book.
Can you find these shapes?

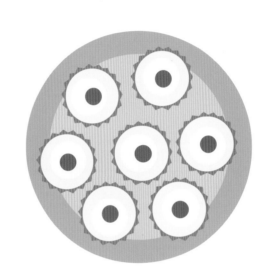

Find these pictures in your book.
Try to answer the questions.

Name the pink circle.

Which circle has a yellow center?

How many squares are in the paintbox?

Which square shows a robot?

Which animal has triangle wings?

How many triangles are in the girl's hair?

Notes for parents and teachers

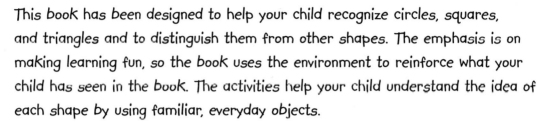

This book has been designed to help your child recognize circles, squares, and triangles and to distinguish them from other shapes. The emphasis is on making learning fun, so the book uses the environment to reinforce what your child has seen in the book. The activities help your child understand the idea of each shape by using familiar, everyday objects.

Sit with your child and read each page to them. Allow time for your child to think about the activity. Encourage them to talk about what they see. Praise your child when they recognize the items shown in the book from their own experience.

Other activities for you to try with your child are:

* Play games such as, "I spy with my little eye something circle/square/triangle shaped that begins with..."

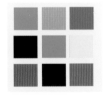

* Cut out pictures of different-shaped objects from a catalog and ask your child to sort them by shape, or to match them to pictures in this book.

* Encourage your child to look for different-shaped objects when you are out and about, or play this game at home.

* Let your child make collages or junk-models of different objects, or mold them in clay, so that they can explore each shape by touch.

Remember to keep it fun. Stop before your child gets tired or loses interest and try again another day. Children learn best when they are relaxed and enjoying themselves. It is best to help them to experience new concepts in small steps, rather than to try to do too much at once.